CULTURE
in Papua New Guinea

Melanie Guile

Chicago, Illinois

For information, address the publisher:
Raintree, 100 N. LaSalle, Suite 1200, Chicago, IL 60602

Printed in China by Wing King Tong.
07 06 05 04 03
10 9 8 7 6 5 4 3 2 1

Library of Congress Cataloging-in-Publication Data
Guile, Melanie.
  Papua New Guinea / Melanie Guile.
      p. cm. -- (Culture in--)
Includes bibliographical references and index.
Contents: Culture in Papua New Guinea -- Performing arts -- Myths,
traditions, and customs -- Costume -- Food -- Women and girls -- Arts
and crafts.
  ISBN 1-4109-0473-3 (library binding)
  1. Papua New Guinea--Civilization--Juvenile literature. [1. Papua New
Guinea--Civilization.] I. Title. II. Series: Guile, Melanie. Culture
in-- .
  DU740.4.G85 2004
  995.3--dc21
                                    2003008587

Acknowledgments
The publisher would like to thank the following for permission to reproduce photographs:
*p. 6 PhotoDisc; pp. 7, 15, 18, 26 Alex Steffe/Lochman Transparencies; pp. 9, 13, 19, 20, 21, 23, 25, 27
Australian Picture Library; pp. 10, 11, 16, 17, 28 All Australian Nature & General; p. 14 Fred Adler; p.
24 Jean-Paul Ferrero/AUSCAPE; p.29 Mathias Kauage, Barrasut Man (Parachute jumper), 1977,
National Gallery of Australia, Canberra, Gordon Darling Fund 1990.*

Other acknowledgments
Cover photograph of the mudmen of Asaro supplied by Australian Picture Library.

CONTENTS

Some words are shown in bold, **like this**. You can find out what they mean by looking in the glossary.

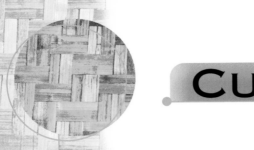

CULTURE IN
Papua New Guinea

Remote and diverse

Some say the people of Papua New Guinea (PNG) came from east Asia about 50,000 years ago. The earliest arrivals moved to land further up the river valleys as later tribes invaded the coast.

For thousands of years these separate tribal groups lived locked away from each other and the outside world. They had no metals, but worked with stone, bone, and wood. There was no writing, but stories about each group's **ancestors** were told in chants and songs passed down through generations. Apart from along the coasts, trade between tribes did not occur. Nature supplied individual groups with all they needed. The people believed that spirits and magical powers provided these things and had to be worshiped with complex **rituals.** The wheel was unknown, so travel was difficult. Many mountain tribes had not been beyond their valley boundaries for centuries. Under these conditions an astonishingly rich and varied culture thrived.

What is culture?

Culture is a people's way of living. It is the way people identify themselves as a group, separate and different from any other. Culture includes a group's language, social customs, and habits, as well as its traditions of art, dance, music, writing, and religion.

In the past Papua New Guineans generally focused on the immediate concerns of their own tribal group. Small tribes lived isolated from one another in **inaccessible** valleys, coastal swamps, or lonely islands. Neighboring **clans** usually spoke different languages and viewed each other as enemies. This meant that each clan's world was small, self-sufficient, and relatively stable. In these conditions thousands of unique cultures developed side by side with very little contact between them.

National flag of
Papua New Guinea

The bird of paradise represents the free
spirit of the people. The five stars of the
Southern Cross, a constellation only visible
in the Southern Hemisphere, show its links
to Australia and other Pacific countries.

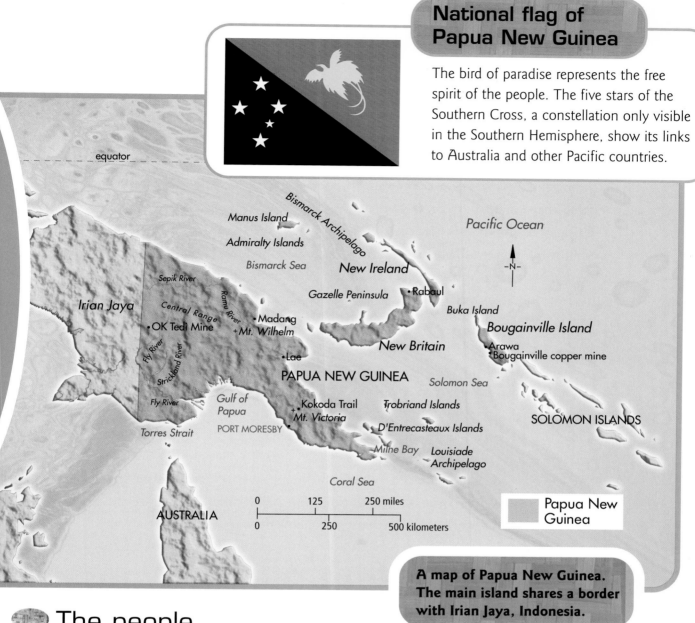

equator

Bismarck Archipelago

Manus Island

Admiralty Islands

Bismarck Sea

Pacific Ocean

New Ireland

Sepik River

Gazelle Peninsula

Rabaul

Ramu River

Irian Jaya

Central Range

Madang

Buka Island

OK Tedi Mine

Mt. Wilhelm

Bougainville Island

Fly River

New Britain

Arawa

Bougainville copper mine

Strickland River

Lae

PAPUA NEW GUINEA

Solomon Sea

Fly River

Gulf of
Papua

Kokoda Trail

Trobriand Islands

Mt. Victoria

SOLOMON ISLANDS

Torres Strait

PORT MORESBY

D'Entrecasteaux Islands

Milne Bay

Louisiade
Archipelago

Coral Sea

-N-

AUSTRALIA

0   125   250 miles

0   250   500 kilometers

Papua New
Guinea

**A map of Papua New Guinea.
The main island shares a border
with Irian Jaya, Indonesia.**

The people

The cultures of Papua New Guinea are among the most diverse in
the world. In 2000 its population was estimated at 4,926,984, made
up of over 1,000 tribal groups speaking over 800 different
languages—over one-third of all the languages in the world. There
are four main **ethnic groups:** the New Guineans in the north, the
Papuans in the south, the Highlanders in the mountainous inland
valleys, and seafaring peoples around the coasts and offshore islands.
Around 85 percent of people live in rural villages and survive on an
average income of $3.23 a day.

Common traditions

In spite of the great diversity of the peoples of PNG, many similar cultural traditions are found throughout the country. For instance, the kinship (*wantok*) system ensures that people always have someone to turn to in tough times. Most tribal groups believe that the natural world is alive with the spirits of **ancestors** who are responsible for good or bad luck. Keeping these spirits content is an important part of everyday life. Another cultural value that is common throughout Papua New Guinea is the importance of strong community ties. Boys and girls are taught the duties and privileges of adulthood during **initiation** ceremonies, and individuals know their role in the overall group. If members leave the community, though, they often begin to question traditional values and lose their strong sense of belonging.

Spiritual life

Almost every aspect of culture in PNG is linked with spiritual beliefs. Beautifully carved ancestor spirit figures stare from the roof pole of the *haus tambaran* (spirit house) to give protection to the inhabitants. Shields made by the Asmats from the Papuan Gulf express the soul of the warrior and are said to make him invincible. During initiation ceremonies in the Sepik River district, elders take on the spiritual power of the ancestors by speaking sacred names. In the North Solomon islands, men blow flutes to summon friendly spirits to important village events.

Spiritual beliefs in PNG culture are commonly expressed in dance.

The *bigman* (chief) holds village ceremonies in the *haus tambaran* (spirit house).

Tough problems

From its rugged landscape to its diverse culture, many aspects of Papua New Guinea are unique and beautiful. However, the country currently faces some serious problems. Some of these problems are especially apparent in cities, where modern and traditional cultures often collide. For example, in Port Moresby, the capital of PNG and its largest city, large **shanty towns** have sprung up, full of people from distant villages who have been unable to find jobs in the city. In contrast to the shanty towns, a few wealthy citizens drive expensive cars and build high fences around their houses to keep out "rascals," a local term for criminals. In an effort to improve the situation, city officials have imposed **curfews** and banned gangs and alcohol. However, the problems of unemployment, poverty, and violent crime are deeply rooted and difficult to solve.

Media

Seventy-two percent of Papua New Guinean people can read and write. There are two daily newspapers in English, and weekly papers in **pidgin** and English. Radios are very popular and there are two national networks. NAU-FM is a private radio station operating in Port Moresby. EM.TV is the only television station in the country, and its music video shows are very popular.

PERFORMING ARTS

Dance, music, and drama are woven together in village **rituals** to pay homage to the spirits. Over 85 percent of Papua New Guineans still follow the ways of their **ancestors,** and traditional dances and songs form a vital part of their culture. However, time has not stood still in PNG. Modern music thrives, particularly in the towns and offshore islands. Rabaul, in the New Britain **archipelago,** was famous as a center for pop and rock music. Unfortunately, Rabaul suffered serious damage after an eruption of the Rabaul Volcano in 1994. Today, studios in Port Moresby produce recordings of local performers, and PNG music is popular all over the Pacific.

Dance

There is an old saying in PNG: "We don't dance for no meaning." Every tribal group has its own dances that accompany important festivals, social events, and spiritual rituals. Dances are held on special occasions such as weddings, funerals, **initiation** ceremonies, and yam harvests. Many songs and dances are based on spiritual beliefs about the ancestors of the village, and costumes represent aspects of them.

In most parts of PNG, dancing sessions go on for many days and nights, sometimes up to six weeks. Ground in the village is cleared and swept, and **rattan** mats are placed around a dancing area. In Oro Province in northeast PNG, the Maisin people begin dancing sessions with a mock duel. The men select the best drummers among them, and as they play, the women arrive beating pots and pans and shouting to distract them. The male drummers refuse to be distracted, though, and the laughing women retreat.

Dances in PNG consist of complex foot and body movements that are performed in sets with short breaks for rests in between. Songs and chants usually accompany dances in PNG and the men and women generally dance together. Some of the words to the songs are so ancient that the meanings have been long forgotten.

Playing with fire

At a cultural festival in the northeastern town of Goroka, Highland women dance with cups of fire on their heads. The other dancers feed the fires with small twigs and leaves to keep them burning.

8

Mudmen of Asaro

The mudmen of Asaro are an eerie sight among the riot of color of the other Highland tribes at cultural festivals *(sing-sings)*. Asaro dancers imitate dead people, donning huge clay masks with hollow, skull–like faces and smearing thick white clay over their bodies to imitate the pale skin of a corpse. They dance slowly, bent over, and flick themselves with twig fly swatters to drive away the imaginary flies attracted to their "dead" flesh. These looming, ghostly costumes are enough to terrify any enemy.

The half-man bush spirit

The dance of the half-man spirit celebrates a Highland myth of a bush spirit with only half a body. Men paint themselves half black, half white, and wear long claws on one hand to mimic the spirit, who lives in the jungle with his half-wife and half-children. Villagers say they know where he has been by the single footprints he leaves behind.

Dancing costumes

Tribes along the Middle Sepik River make elaborate masked costumes (*tumbuan*) for ceremonial dances. The men smear mud over turtle or coconut shells to form the masks, then paint them with colored clay or charcoal. They decorate the masks with shells, pig tusks, and feathers from a cassowary, a bird common in Papua New Guinea. Instead of wearing the masks on their faces, the dancers lash them to a cone-shaped frame. The frame is covered with flowers, leaves, and a **raffia** skirt at the base. The dancer gets inside the frame and moves it to the beat of the dance.

Every tribal group in PNG has its own dances to accompany important events.

Traditional music

Drums, flutes, and wooden horns are used in traditional **rituals** all over PNG. In Tangu, in the Madang district, gongs are used to announce community events. Everyone in the village has their own gong signal, and important information is communicated through these percussion instruments. Eastern Highland men blow flutes both as a symbol of male power and to call up spirits. The Gimi people (also from the eastern Highlands) play flutes at boys' **initiations** and pig festivals. Women are not permitted to see these sacred instruments.

Papua New Guineans consider flutes sacred instruments, used to call up spirits.

Modern music

PNG has some of the most popular bands in the Pacific. PNG pop music is a mix of **indigenous** rhythms and reggae sounds, often with a hint of edgier rock. It is a rough sound with lots of percussion and electric guitar. Lyrics are in **pidgin** or English and have themes like love, religion, and growing up. String bands are hugely popular throughout the Pacific region, and some of the best come from PNG. With acoustic guitars, ukuleles, and added electric instruments, string bands have a country-and-western sound. Though it is no longer active, the most famous string band in PNG was the Moab String band led by the hugely popular singer-songwriter George Telek.

There is a thriving music industry in PNG. Before the destructive eruption of the Rabaul Volcano in 1994, Rabaul was home to all of the major recording studios. Now based in Port Moresby, Papua New Guinean recording companies produce over 90 percent of the recordings played in the country. The same companies also produce music videos, which are featured on EM.TV, the only television channel in PNG.

MYTHS,
Traditions, and Customs

Ancient and modern

Papua New Guinea has a tribal culture. Around 85 percent of the people still live traditional lives, farming and hunting for food and maintaining the spiritual beliefs and customs of their **ancestors.** Although 97 percent of the population is **Christian** and every village has its own church and pastor, the ancient tribal myths and **rituals** survive alongside this faith. Keeping **ancestral** spirits happy is considered vital to the well-being of a village. People attribute any sickness or bad luck to an evil influence, such as witchcraft or **sorcery,** and spiritual healers are as important as doctors.

For many generations, strong cultural beliefs helped keep communities together. Now, however, these ties are loosening. Unemployment has led many young men to migrate to cities like Lae and Port Moresby for work. There they live in squalid **shanty towns** with no support from village elders, competing for the few available jobs.

Power and status

Displaying one's wealth and power is an important aspect of PNG culture. *Kina* shells are still worn by well-off tribespeople to show how rich they are. Highland *bigmen* (chiefs) show their status by giving extravagant gifts to friends and rivals at *moga* ceremonies—although they expect to receive equally costly gifts or favors in return! Valuable boar tusks decorate the houses of the wealthiest families in Highland villages, and *bigmen* will marry as many women as they can afford (wives are purchased from their families by paying a **bride price**).

Perhaps because of their traditional interest in material wealth, many tribes have adapted well to Western styles of commerce. Members of the Highland and Milne Bay tribes are good business people, and keep a shrewd eye out for opportunities to make money from tourists. Handicrafts made for the tourist trade have brought much-needed cash to many remote communities.

Wantok

Wantok is **pidgin** for "one talk," and it refers to people who speak the same language. *Wantoks* are members of the same **clan** and must be loyal to one another. Food, houses, and jobs are shared, and members of the clan help each other out. However, the system also lends itself to **corruption.** Powerful *bigmen* favor their *wantoks* when distributing wealth, and politicians are more likely to give the best jobs and the highest salaries to their *wantoks*. Even the courts can be corrupted, and judges sometimes let their *wantoks* off lightly.

Wealthy tribespeople wear *kina* shells around their necks to show their status.

Malangan funeral rites

The Malangan people of remote New Ireland carve life-size figures of the dead as part of their funeral ceremonies. Depending on the clan, bodies may be buried, burned, or set adrift in a boat. The dead person's soul is said to cross into the ancestors' world with the help of spirits, and the carved image is displayed at the funeral feast.

The payback system

For thousands of years, the traditional payback system has been a way of life for most tribespeople in PNG. Payback is an "eye for an eye, tooth for a tooth" system of justice. It means that any injury, death, or harm caused must be avenged in the same manner. Unfortunately, sometimes acts of revenge occur even if the harm is accidental or suspected rather than real. The payback system can result in feuds between tribes that last for years and cost many lives. Payback is not considered acceptable by the official justice system in Papua New Guinea, but police officers are often unable to prevent **clans** from taking their revenge, and tribal loyalties can cause officials to turn a blind eye to payback-related crimes. Today money is often acceptable as a peace offering, but payback violence is still common in some areas.

Traditionally, the heads captured by headhunters were thought to have magical properties.

Human prizes

Fifty years ago many tribespeople on the main island of PNG were cannibals and headhunters. Young Highland warriors would raid neighboring clans in order to capture heads, which would then be smoked over a fire to preserve them, or hung up on skull racks inside their houses. The tribespeople believed that heads contained powerful magic and brought protection from evil to those in the village. Sometimes the bodies of dead family members would be eaten as a sign of love and respect, and the bones preserved for good luck.

Even today, Highlanders wear the bones of relatives as part of their traditional clothing to keep the spirits of loved ones near them. Although headhunting has been outlawed, there are rumors that some tribespeople still continue the practice.

Growing up

In traditional PNG culture, there is no such thing as **adolescence.** Young teenagers are regarded as children until they complete their **rituals** of **initiation.** Boys' initiations are very elaborate and are taken extremely seriously. The exact type of ritual varies from region to region, but all involve some sort of ordeal or task, such as spending weeks in the jungle alone or planting a field of yams.

In the Sepik River district, initiation lasts an entire month. First, boys undergo an hour-long ceremony in which their bodies are cut with a bamboo blade to create hundreds of small scars. These represent the scales of the crocodile, the tribe's **totem**, which is thought to enter the boys' souls to guide them through life. When the initiation is complete, the boys are given the responsibilities of men.

Sky world myths

Many tribal groups in PNG believe in a sky world. The inland Ayon people tell stories about a sky man, Tumbrenjak, who climbed down to Earth to hunt and could not get back because his rope ladder was cut down; he became the father of all human beings. The Keraki Papuans on the southwest coast believe that a heavy rain means that the sky world's inhabitants are angry. These Papuans look up anxiously in case the **rattan** floor of the sky world collapses from the excess water.

15

COSTUME

Living art

Like many aspects of life in PNG, the art of traditional dress and body decoration expresses important aspects of a person's identity. Tribespeople pay careful attention to the colors and designs of another person's face paint and tattoos, or to the kinds of feathers worn in a headdress. All of these things send a message about a person's home district, tribe, wealth, status in the village, and so on. For this reason, body decoration is highly developed in PNG, especially in the Highlands where traditional culture remains strong.

For *sing-sings* (cultural festivals), tribal groups spend hours preparing spectacular costumes.

Tribal dress

There are three main parts to each Highland tribal costume: the headdress, face and body paint, and ornaments. Headdresses consist of wigs made of human hair or plant fiber and decorated with flowers, leaves, and feathers. The colors and patterns of the face paint indicate the wearer's tribe and status. Jewelry made of shells, tusks, and strings of dogs' teeth show the person's wealth. Headbands of blue-green beetles are often worn and capes of opossum fur are draped around the neck. Men and women wear the same basic costumes, but those of men are more richly decorated.

The costume of each tribe has its own distinctive features. Huli men from the southern Highlands are famous for their elaborate and beautiful wigs. Young men dressed for the bachelor dance wear yellow, red, and blue face paint, and a large wig of human hair decorated with the feathers of parrots and birds of paradise.

Colors and patterns of face paint show the wearer's tribe and status.

Face paint

Face and body painting is traditional in the Highlands. Tribespeople make the colored paints using natural materials, including charcoal, powdered seashells, vegetable dyes, and yellow, red, and white clays. First, the skin is oiled to create a good base, and then the **pigment** is applied with a brush made from the chewed end of a stick. It can take many hours to paint the complex designs, and the whole family helps. For important events like the Highland *sing-sings*, people often buy store-bought paints because they are easier to use and come in a wide range of colors. White correction fluid is becoming popular as a face paint, but the brush does not produce as fine a line as the traditional twig.

Not long ago the Huli were feared cannibals in the Tari Highlands. Young men would be sent alone into the jungle to learn bush skills and prepare for manhood. They would begin to grow their hair in preparation for making their first wig, a symbol of their coming-of-age and their readiness for war.

Modern dress

When not in costume for traditional celebrations, almost everyone in PNG wears secondhand Western clothing, often originally from Australia. Traveling merchants buy old clothes in bulk and sell them in the villages.

Menswear

Traditionally, Highland men wore only a belt woven from plant fibers and a **sheath** to cover their genitals made from the hardened skin of a kind of squash. Theses sheaths are still worn on ceremonial occasions and are highly prized by tourists as souvenirs. Today, though, Western fashions are more common. Young men in particular favor denim jackets and tie red bandanas around their foreheads. T-shirts printed with religious sayings are also popular.

Jewelry

Bilas (jewelry) is a **pidgin** word meaning "flash." Wearing costly ornaments has long been an important way for a family to show its wealth and status in PNG, and it still is. Before Europeans came to the main island, shells were used as a form of money. Gold-lipped pearl shells were carved into curved shapes called *kina* and traded for valuable goods. Circles of smaller shells called *toea* were like coins and were often worn through the nose or as necklaces. These words survive today in PNG's paper currency. 100 *toea* coins equal 1 *kina*, and real shells are often used as money in ceremonies such as weddings.

Every body ornament has meaning. Strings of teeth from dogs, porpoises, or fruit bats indicate a person's wealth. *Bigmen* wear *kina* around their necks to show their status and power. Human bones are also sometimes worn, either as necklaces and bracelets or through the nose. These may be the bones of deceased relatives, whose spirits are believed to linger in their remains. Although 97 percent of the population of PNG is **Christian,** ancient beliefs remain strong throughout the country.

Shells are highly valued for traditional costumes.

Tattoos

In Manus Island, off the southeast coast of the mainland, body tattoos are common. Once they were applied to both women and men by painfully puncturing the skin with sharpened wood or bone needles coated with dye. Only people of high status were permitted to have tattoos. Girls and women were tattooed at special stages of their lives, and also when a male relative safely returned from a sea voyage. Today you can still see full-body tattoos on older women, but felt pen is used as a painless and temporary alternative for special occasions.

Tattoos were traditionally applied by inserting dye under the skin using sharp needles. Today, felt-tip pens or paint are often used instead.

Sing-sing cultural festivals

For two days and nights in September, the sports arena at Goroka becomes a living sea of color. Over 20,000 men and women gather in traditional costume to compete for cash prizes. The event is so thrilling that tourists and photographers come from all over the world to enjoy the scene.

FOOD

Traditional food

The traditional staple foods in PNG, yam (*kaukau*) and sago, are starchy and bland. They fill empty stomachs quickly but are not very nourishing. Yams were brought to PNG long ago by Spanish traders from South America. Most meals are made from fresh ingredients available locally, including vegetables from village gardens; fruits like mango, banana, and coconuts; and fish, opossum, wild birds, and a type of animal known as a tree kangaroo. Most village families own a pig or chickens, but these are regarded as a form of wealth and only eaten at special feasts (*mumu*) held for weddings or funerals. Today's villagers have access to canned and dried Western foods, but they are very expensive.

A Trobriand Island villager stacks yams in a village compound during a yam harvest festival.

Yams

The root vegetable *kaukau* is a kind of yam, and is grown in village vegetable gardens throughout PNG, except in the lowlands. Growing yams is an important part of village life, especially for men, and good *kaukau* farmers earn great respect. Ceremonies and celebrations accompany the yam harvest, with a procession through the village to the yam house where the roots are stored. In the Highlands yams are part of every meal. They are usually roasted in the fire or boiled, and can be served as a savory meal with green vegetables from the women's gardens or sweetened with sticks of sugarcane.

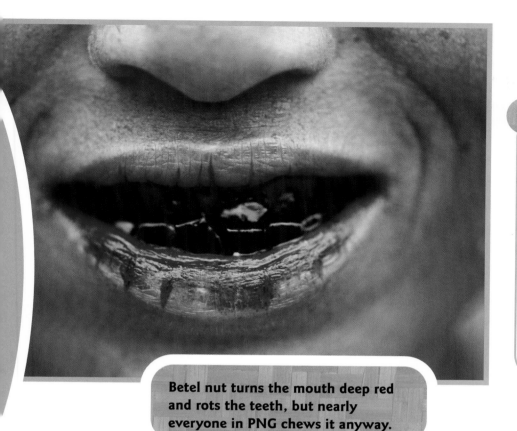

Jawbreakers

If you crave a snack in PNG, you can always nibble on a Kundu cracker. These rock-hard crackers were first brought to PNG by British sailors early last century. Today Kundu brand crackers are famous and sold all over the country.

Betel nut turns the mouth deep red and rots the teeth, but nearly everyone in PNG chews it anyway.

Sago

Sago is a food made from the soft bark of the sago palm tree. It is a native plant that grows in the lowlands where soils are too poor and swampy to grow yams. The women spend many hours stripping the bark, soaking it in water, and beating it to remove the bitter taste. The pithy bark turns into a white flour that is cooked and eaten with vegetables. Coastal people in PNG eat a greater variety of food, including many different types of fish, lobsters, and crabs. These are often flavored with coconut milk and spices such as ginger and nutmeg, traded from nearby Indonesia.

Betel nut

Betel nut (*buai*) is the acorn-sized nut of a palm tree. Similar to coffee, it is a mild **stimulant,** and just about everyone aged five and up in PNG chews it. The nut is peeled and chewed together with mustard stick and powder made of crushed coral. Chewing betel nut this way creates lots of saliva, and locals constantly eject streams of bright red spit. Some city buildings, like airports and hospitals, have established "no-spit" zones. *Buai* turns the mouth and tongue deep red and rots the teeth, but nevertheless it is hugely popular throughout the country.

WOMEN AND GIRLS

Women's work

Women look after their children, do household chores, cook all the meals, carry water, and tend the vegetable gardens. Many women also produce crafts to sell to tourists in market towns for a few dollars. A married woman must obey her husband and eldest sons. It is considered wrong for a woman to approach a man to talk to him, or to eat at the same table, even with male members of her own family. In the villages men and women generally live separately in special men's and women's houses.

Second best

It is not easy being a woman in PNG. Although all women are allowed to vote, and the country's laws make it illegal to discrimate against them, women are treated as second best in almost every part of the country. In the past tribal customs generally helped to protect women and girls from harm. Now the old ways are breaking down, especially among the young men who leave the villages to seek work in towns. The weakening of the village social system has resulted in more violence against women and girls.

Marriage

Women are expected to marry young and have children right away. When a girl reaches the age of sixteen, she is considered ready for marriage and must be bought by a groom with a **bride price.** This is usually paid with pigs or chickens, which are a form of wealth in PNG. The bride price is set by the girl's father and it is often very high. If a young man likes a girl he must pay this price before he can marry, and it can take many years of working and saving. In some parts of the country, men have more than one wife, which can cause tension in the family.

Human currency

Young girls are sometimes offered as compensation in tribal disputes. In 1998 the Jimi clan in Western Highland Province offered two teenage girls as payment to settle a fight. The National Court in PNG ordered an investigation and the girls were returned to their village.

Women carry their babies in a *bilum*, which is a handmade string bag slung over the shoulder or forehead. Leaves, bark, or rags are used in place of diapers.

Women's and children's health

Although there is a national health care system in PNG, its hospitals often do not have adequate supplies and equipment, and there is a shortage of highly trained doctors. For this reason many women die during childbirth, and an increasing number of newborn babies do not survive. Over 60 out of every 1,000 children born in PNG do not live to their first birthday. One-third of babies who do survive do not get enough to eat. A small number of women's clinics are run by churches and aid organizations, but they reach only a tiny fraction of the women who need help.

A brighter picture

The situation of women in PNG is not all negative. Sixty-three percent of women in PNG can read and write. Although there are 15 percent fewer girls in primary school than boys, the gap is narrowing. National laws protect women's rights, and courts often overturn unfair judgments against women made by local village councils. The constitution guarantees women equal property, marriage, and family rights, and there is a government Office of Women's Affairs in Port Moresby dedicated to improving women's place in PNG society. There are even women working in high-level government and business jobs.

At the village level, the tightly knit community serves as a support system for women. Every woman looks out for the children and cares for old or sick people, so the burden of this kind of work is shared. Women and children participate in village celebrations, dancing through the night alongside the men. However, most musical instruments are *tabu* (forbidden) to women, who must not even look at a flute being played. If they do, the spirit being summoned may refuse to come.

In the Trobriand Islands, off the east coast of the mainland, the **Polynesian** culture is **matrilineal,** which means all property is passed down to the female side of the family. Male chiefs still control the islands, but the women's property rights mean they have some power and are treated with respect.

Along with taking care of her house and children, this woman from the Sepik area makes traditional masks to sell to tourists.

There are fewer girls than boys in primary schools in PNG, but the gap is narrowing.

Women speaking out

Between 1988 and 1997, the people of Bougainville, an island off of mainland Papua New Guinea, fought for their independence from PNG, a conflict that claimed 20,000 lives. Bougainville authorities were eventually given a larger degree of power, although the dispute still has not been fully settled. In March 1999 on International Women's Day, more than 700 women held a rally in the capital, Arawa, to proclaim their commitment to peace and independence. Speakers at the rally called on the national government to recognize the rights of women and of the people of Bougainville to rule themselves.

Witch-hunt

In the Eastern Highlands of PNG, bad luck, illness, or sudden death are often blamed on *sangumas,* or witches. Women accused of witchcraft are sometimes hurt or even killed by villagers who believe they have sent evil spirits against them. Old or unmarried women are the most likely to be accused.

ARTS AND CRAFTS

Art in life

Art is part of everyday life in Papua New Guinea. Carvings, decorations, and paintings are made to express key aspects of the social and spiritual lives of the villagers. Beautiful carvings on their houses represent the spirits of **ancestors** who guard the buildings. Brilliant colors painted on faces and bodies indicate the **clan** and status of dancers. Ghostly masks and images painted on shields and weapons are intended to frighten away enemies and give power to the owner. The highly skilled artists and craftspeople who make these things are proud of the work they do to express the values of the community and the power of the spirit world.

Wooden carvings express important aspects of the social and spiritual lives of villagers in PNG.

Masks

Traditional masks are made to represent ancestors and spirits and are used for important ceremonies. Those made without eyeholes are not worn but displayed on the prows of boats or in spirit houses called *haus tambaran*. These masks are carved from wood or made from turtle shells, and decorated with teeth, plant fibers, and shells. Life-size woven **rattan** figures called *tumbuan* represent the spirit of creation or the spirit of the clan. Some *tumbuan* are so sacred they are brought out only once a year at special **rituals.**

Savi (which means "power" or "knowledge" in **pidgin**) are the most powerful masks, and only the *bigmen* (chiefs) may handle them. They attract **ancestral** spirits and are displayed in important places, such as on the steep peaks of houses and in the *haus tambaran*. *Savi* masks are easy to recognize because they depict faces with aggressively stuck-out tongues. *Mai* masks are worn by the teachers in boys' **initiation** ceremonies. Other masks might be worn as charms to bring luck during a hunt.

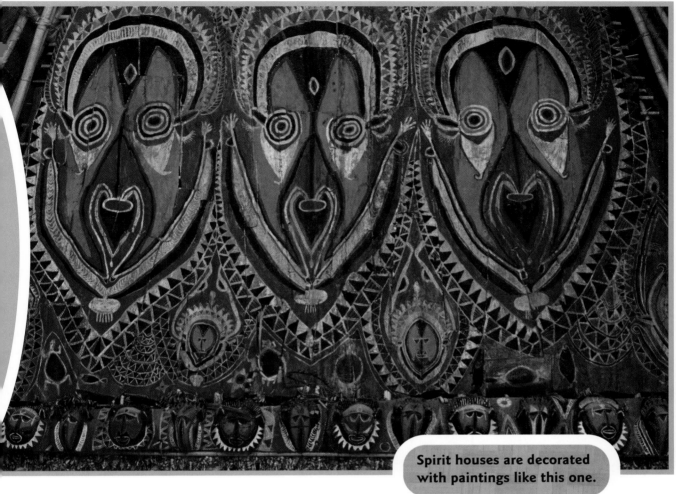

Skull racks

Tribespeople traditionally decorated the skulls of relatives and enemies killed in battle and placed them on elaborately carved skull racks. They carved skull racks in the shape of human figures, then painted and decorated them. The skulls were hung with grass string or piled on a shelf. Although headhunting is no longer legal, the skull racks themselves, hoisted high in the men's houses, are still an amazing sight.

Spirit boards

Spirit boards, also called story boards, are sacred objects made by people of the Gulf of Papua. Originally made of beaten bark, tribespeople painted them with protective spirits and then hung them in men's and women's huts. Spirit boards were believed to ward off evil spirits and sickness, tell the future, and predict the outcome of wars. Now carved and painted on wood, not bark, they are produced in large numbers for the tourist trade. Even today they are considered excellent examples of fine Papua New Guinean art.

Crafts

Bowls carved in the shape of fish are typical of the crafts made by the Trobriand Islanders. Known for their wood carving throughout PNG, the islanders also make items for the tourist trade, such as furniture shaped like animals and walking sticks. Their carvings are often inlaid with mother-of-pearl and are greatly prized.

Traditional coil pots, made by molding snakes of clay into vessels, are made by the people of Aibom on the Sepik River. Their distinctive pottery is decorated with faces painted in white.

Braided and woven grass belts are part of traditional dress in the Highlands. Incredibly intricate designs are woven and knotted into these belts, which are often decorated with leaves and bark. Bougainville Island is the home of the famous *buka* basket weavers, considered the best in Papua New Guinea.

Weapons

Weapons were once considered sacred by the warriors who depended on them in battle. Warriors made daggers out of bone or stone and sharpened them to a fierce point. The blades of swords were embedded with sharks' teeth. Shield making was considered a sacred act, because warriors believed that a spirit inside each shield would offer protection during battle. The Asmat shield makers of the Gulf of Papua are said to be the finest in the world, and examples of their craftsmanship hang in galleries around the world.

A traditional axe, made from sharpened stone, wood, and woven grass

This stencil by Mathias Kauage is called *Barrasut Man (Parachute Jumper)*.

Modern art

Not all of PNG's art is purely traditional. The few who are able to afford a university education can study painting at the University of Papua New Guinea in Port Moresby. A number of modern artists, such as Mathias Kauage and Gickmai Kundun, have gained international reputations.

Sculptor Gickmai Kundun is one of the country's most respected modern artists. He prefers to work with scrap metal he finds, such as rusty parts of old cars. His style is deliberately rough and unpolished in order to emphasize that it is handmade. Although Kundun is often inspired by traditional stories, he also expresses modern ideas in his sculptures. A work exhibited at the Port Moresby Art School in the 1990s was called *Nuclear Testing in the Pacific* and was intended as a protest against **nuclear weapons.**

GLOSSARY

adolescence stage in life when a person is no longer thought of as a child, but is not yet considered an adult

ancestor person from whom one is descended

ancestral relating to the people from whom one is descended

archipelago group of islands

bride price price set by a young woman's family that a man must pay in order to marry her

cannibalism practice of eating human flesh

Christian having to do with or following Christianity, a religion based on the belief in one god and the teachings of Jesus, as written in a holy book called the Bible

clan family or tribal group

corruption dishonest or criminal activities by government officials or other powerful people, usually for personal gain

curfew set time at which the citizens of a community must not be outdoors

ethnic group people who share a specific culture, language, and background

inaccessible impossible to reach

indigenous original or native to a particular country or area

initiation ceremony to mark an important stage in a person's life

kina type of shell traditionally worn as jewelry by Papua New Guineans as a sign of wealth. Today, the *kina* is also the name for the Papua New Guinean form of money.

matrilineal social system in which property and wealth are passed from mother to daughter

nuclear weapon missile or bomb with massive explosive power based on nuclear fission, the splitting of an atom's nucleus into smaller fragments

pidgin simple language introduced by European traders to communicate with tribal groups in Papua New Guinea; or, any simple language used by people who speak different languages to communicate

pigment substance, such as a paint or dye, used to give color to other materials

Polynesian relating to the region that includes many islands and island groups located in the South Pacific Ocean, including the Hawaiian Islands, Easter Island, Samoa, and French Polynesia

raffia palm-leaf fiber used for making hats, baskets, skirts, and so on

rattan stiff material made from woven palm leaves

ritual religious tradition or ceremony

shanty town very poor community of roughly built shacks

sheath close-fitting cover

sorcery witchcraft

stimulant drug that gives the user extra energy for a short time

totem symbol (often an animal) of a clan, family, or group; or a carved image of such a symbol

FURTHER
Reading

Dalal, Anita. *Myths of Oceania.* Chicago: Raintree, 2002.

Franklin, Sharon and others. *Southwest Pacific: Understanding Geography and History Through Art.* Chicago: Raintree, 1999.

Gascoigne, Ingrid. *Papua New Guinea.* Tarrytown, N.Y.: Marshall Cavendish, 1998.

Malnic, Jutta, and John Kasaipwalova. *Kula: Myth and Magic in the Trobriand Islands.* Wahroonga, New South Wales, Australia: Cowrie Books, 2000.

INDEX